WHY DANCE?

R. Nikolas Macioci

ISBN: 1-7349469-1-8
ISBN-13: 978-1-7349469-1-8

FOR MOM and CHARLES

Table of Contents

I

WHY DANCE?

Great floor-to-ceiling windows scowl night in.
Frost scrawls cold stars on the glass, needlepoints
a tapestry for short days, long nights. Suspended
lanterns oscillate. A peacock tail of color fans
across the polished floor. The dance seems dreamwoven,
so naturally does it move through the dancers'
bodies, giving the room itself a facsimile
of life. The dance asks them to trust, to give
no urgent reply, just to move and be removed
by a discreet waltz. Arms warm against another's,
eyes wondering without knowing. The minute
scraping of feet is masked beneath scattered talk
and violins. The dancers part, give up
the closeness that holds gestures to a minimum,
and drift in opposite directions to seek
intervals when they can lean on the eyes of others.
This is when each waits for someone else
who has never had a name until now,
whose face, sweet as dawn, shiny with touchable
sweat, scatters away the personal silence
with an invitation. The partners encircle
each other with vague desires and begin again
the wordless discussion, the urgent gaze
of wordless questions. For them, the answer
is in being able to take the unfamiliar
into their arms, to vanish beyond the known,
to exist for a few moments for some
useless, intoxicated reason.

SYMPATHY FOR WOMEN WHO STRUGGLE AGAINST MEN AND MORTALITY FOR A MOMENT OF TENDERNESS

Whiter than sky or moon or God's arms,
the sheets we lie on cradle our intimacy.
How wise that we would practice love
before death makes a joke of us.
In this way, we keep each other
from absences. You guard my skin against
the cold, keep my smile against your cheek
in the bedroom darkness. How shall we fill
our hearts? How shall we begin to manage
the shine of the moon on our throats,
the embrace of emptiness even
as you ask again for the silk
inward path to me? Our passion
is phony. Eventually
you take everything. Of course you do.
I am a woman, and what shall I do
but rage and wrap my dreams around the shine
of your sweat and cry, "Oh," and weigh against
your fickle crotch and occasionally
catch a glimpse of the inevitable
when you rise to smoke a cigarette,
and I roll toward the window to see
if there are any more lost people
in raincoats on the summer street below us

DESIRED IMAGE

A swimmer, an apparition in red
trunks, shimmering, a look of love glaring
off his skin, splinters light as he walks
toward the shoreline. She wants to cry out
about desire, to remove her eyes, but
she can't. She darts yet another look,
praises him, wonders about how to renounce hope,
delusion, the feathery feeling
in her thighs. She dreams the fulfillment
of caresses will come up like a soft wind,
take her in its arms laden with fable,
lean her back to burn over the void of sand.

When he rises from the foam, wet stars fall
from his shoulders. His slight wobble mirrors
her vertigo. He sees her, hurls a look
that falls on her like death. At the same time
she winces at a scar on his forehead
she hadn't seen before. She takes pleasure
in his wound. Her fingertips touch her own
face, search for perfection. When she looks
again, he stumbles in the surf. She finds
the mole on her cheek, and he becomes her
diminished equal.

She stands, brushes sand from her legs,
folds her beach towel, almost forgetting to
take a last look at the sea, at his image
disappearing from her mind like
a sensation of imagined beauty.

DARING TO DIVE

We sit and talk of plans and poetry.
I watch my hands settle in my lap, look
at your face that does not suspect
the slightest preparation for my dive.

In my head, an ocean unfurls. Waves
peak and beach. I taste salty air and sweat,
assess the current, the roll of the tide,
the unreasoning will to ripple
in mid-air, knowing how the distance down
can deceive.

Nonetheless, tree high, arms out, spine curved,
head aimed, sharp as an eggshell, I fall,
translucent as early morning, my body
spearing watery blue down to where
affection fills my lungs and sharks tear flesh
before bones can reach the surface.
From my abundant silence you do not detect
the nearness of a drowning.

THE WAITER AT LAKE LOUISE

His Nordic bone structure strains
beneath sunburned skin, his beauty
the artistry of birthright. He
is as lean as a lifeguard,
and his head comes close to touching
the top of the doorway
on his many trips to and from the kitchen.

Four of us are seated for dinner
around a white linen table cloth.
The waiter bends over our shoulders
to fill water glasses. Pretending
to watch the ice swirl in oncoming currents,
each of us steals a piece of his perfection
with a glance. He places the silverware,
leaves menus, becomes more beautiful as
he turns away, and lantern light burnishes
his cheeks and glows pink on the thin layer
of sweat glossing his face.

Waiting for him to return with the wine,
we take refuge in small talk, refusing
each other's eyes and the truth his youth
taunts us with. We spurt shallow laughter,
hide real words. Becoming red-faced
from drink, we could brush politeness aside
and say how naked we feel sitting there,
middle-aged, in a silence of body
that talks louder than the polite words
we bandy, but we don't skin ourselves open
to that exposure of desire below the surface.

We simply wait, and he returns
balanced on the edge of our peripheral
sensitivity, speaking to each of us
in turn, taking our orders as we
continue to talk appropriately,
suspecting his presence is the ghost
of repression that separates
passion from respectability.

THE GAMEKEEPER OBSERVES HIS SLEEPING WIFE

A quail feather
flickers to the ground.
It's a golden leaf in the twilight found
as I shut a book and stand at the window.
The mantle clock swells with time, releases the hour's metallic
sound.
You sit in a tall chair, your eyes half-closing more and more.
The sewing in your lap, washed in early firelight,
slips into restless shadows on the floor.
You shift. Your womanly hands stir,
pull the firelight closer,
until it is skin tight
around your shoulders.

BREAKFAST AND SHAME

My hands close over your arms, skim
your blood. We copy each other's gaze,
the skin between us ready to disappear.
On the bed, our shadows raise sails
of insuperable warmth charted
directly at expanding trust. Our clothes,
snagged on furniture edges, watch and know
the truth. Your mouth floods my tongue with
aftertaste of cigarette smoke. A sock on the floor
somehow connects us to the universe.

The smallest light begins to fill our coffee
cups. You pull a robe shut, civilized, sit straight,
and assess. It is the Edwardian way.
I tap crumbs from a slice of toast, pat
napkins perfectly into place, sip orange
juice, thinking I'd rather be in my own house
now, embarrassed by the memory
of drawing your head against my chest. You
hand me my hat and a look that says our
passion has been mostly drunk with mistakes.

RAIN IS OUR SIGNIFICANCE

its watery impression dapples
your hands, and I am silkened too
by its limpid reflections. Our skins
fill with mottled evidence that night
has flung on a silver mantle and stands
outside our window watching us. Ghosts
of its existence, like satin bubbles,
wash down our walls. It sees everything
in this room, looks at us on the bedclothes
of spring, holds us in its luminous clasp.
We brim with its hidden waters. Its
wetness drenches our lips. The room sparkles
in slow motion. Rivulets run off
our shoulders. On the bed, shadows
of our bodies pool. Mercurial
drops roll down the window to their futures,
oracles rounded by streetlight. By dawn
we can barely see their teethmark-touches,
spars of rain we have borrowed
from this rented room.

THE OKINAWA NUDES

Perhaps I should not admit the pleasure
I found in taking my uncle's photo
album from the plywood darkness below
a shelf of wine glasses. My composure,
at nine, melted each time the exposure
of flesh met my eye. Their beauty was so
uncomplicated, three girls in shadow,
seen bathing, breasts raised toward sun like treasure.
An authentic souvenir of the war,
the photo was not an embarrassment,
but pure balance between art and honor.
I never once felt less than innocent
looking into those fragile faces for
signs of how, amid death, their days were spent.

BOWFOX ROAD

The sky, scabbed with clouds, is almost human,
nothing more than bare skin, blue as a bent
cornflower, but blotched with dark clouds you think
are too tight with rain to last another minute.
Bending on each knee, I smell the road dust,
the coming rain as I pick knots from shoestrings
that settle in loops on my fingers

Rising on the berm of the gravel road,
you surprise me with assorted smiles, lead
into a tangle of woods bonneted
by an over-warmth of staring sun.
We lift and push clothes from our adolescence,
listen for the occasional car, the throbbing
green around us sticky with insect hums.
We trim each other with silent touches,
curiousity. From a twist of hair, from hips
that hold steady the balance to quickness
drawing inner shrieks from flowering bones,
our heads fill with smooth pieces of light
and mossy fragrances from the forest floor.
When the clouds finally break, we are dressed
again, bent on returning to the road,
the shine of rain on a thousand elm leaves.

PREY

They have only mistakes and the lush heat
of early spring rolling awake beside them.
He sprawls, stretches. Sounds of indigestion
lazily mar his beauty. She listens
for the hum of his first thought.
He swings his legs from the bed, his first move
in dissolving time and place. She watches him
swat flies from the sunrise, dreading
the taloned beast he must seem to them,
mouth ajar, jaws darkened by thick stubble.
She tests the air for bitterness or joy,
follows his sweet scent to the window
where he is looking at great clouds of sun,
and she knows in the pit of her stomach
as she loops her arm around his middle,
that he envisions better places.
With the odor of blood on his breath, he
is ready to leap away from this kill.
Cold sweat on his back speaks of his
indifference, tells her to remove her arm.
She piles on clothes, imagining him
leaping out the window into twigs
bursting with new light, his suicidal bones
filling the branches with love's mockery

She returns to the bed to straighten
the ocean of sky they slept on, smoothing
indifferent sheets smeared with the burns
of unmanned stars.

SNOW TALK

Silence recalls shared reason for failure.
Our time falls away over the bleak rim of winter.
In the February air,
warnings freeze around us, and
a hard moment of searching is a pretense.
Pushing fingers toward the bottom,
we pocket our warmth. Our chances,
like the snow, go on falling.
We fumble away from each other,
hearts tightened by mind-darkening truth.

A PRIVATE BURN

In kitchen darkness, I pocket matches
to carry downstairs to a far corner
of the basement. At the workbench, I
pick up an empty Planter's can saved
for mixing paint and place it
on the cement floor, thinking it will be
a safe spot to dispose of old love. I found
your letters today, heart's death coming back
to me as I bent over memories
I found in a cardboard box
when I closeted Christmas ornaments.
On my knees, I unfist the first letters,
their kindness, their deceptive ease, everything
that should have forecast the consequence
of obvious charm. Your best assets
ignite now. Your suave, reassuring lies
flame up, the luminous flesh of paper
turning stiff and white from the freeze of fire,
your commitment buried in great waves
of incineration, your sentiments falling to
ash too brittle to be carried upstairs.

AUTUMN: A FURTIVE PLEASURE

I swallow autumn's kiss,
its tongue hot from summer.
Haunted leaves at my neck
lick my skin, open a rustle
of red embraces. I stretch out
on the breeze, limbs wrapped around
the fever of a pin oak,
the shine of sumac. I dare to need
October against my chest,
November's breath teaching me
to regret how carefully
I learned to conceal passion.

JANUARY VISIT

A man rings a bell on the bitter cold. He
stomps his shoes on the doorstep, snowdust flies
into the dark, each flake a lightning,
a piece of shattered shoe print. He makes
warmth in his skull by thinking of fire.

She opens the door on the third ring,
coffee cup in hand, her last swallow
still warm as the breath in her throat. She speaks
to him by name. Happy that she has answered
the ring, he closes the distance between them
a step, says that he has brought provisions

for this frozen night, and won't she
let him come in to melt the sting of cold
from his skin, to share the coffee pot
he sees behind her.
She stands aside, and he
enters her house.

She does not pour coffee over his hands
for warmth or revenge. To free him of winter,
she climbs the stairs, pulls back covers,
and piles blankets on an old passion
that begins with ice.

A HISTORY OF LOVE

In the first grade and terrorstruck,
I nimbly jumped from square to chalked square,
consenting to play a girl's game which seemed
as pure as white lines on the sidewalk.
When I raised my head to see into the sun,
her hair streamed yellow to gleaming ends as
she waited for her turn at the opposite end
of the grid. Straddling the center number,
bent at the waist, I skimmed the sliver of chalk
across spring air, missing the targeted square
by an inch. When it was her turn, I watched
her feet make order of a numbered sequence,
hopping from foot to foot, summing up success
at the other end. She shrugged off her conquest
with an ingenuous smile. I studied her as
she re-chalked the lines, learned to want
new language to express the weight of desire
slicing my heart's underside with heat
and glimmerings as sacred as first snow.

At Barret Junior High, my bones grew
past sleeve length. I became shy of what I wanted
to say to one particular girl and
exceedingly awful at walking home
beside her. It took many tries for me
to lift those heavy books away from her
and become the moderate-sized knight
shouldering the responsibility
for her walk home. I suffered without cure
when we touched accidently, jolted
together by the uneven sidewalk.
I said mostly nothing. When words left my mouth,
they hung above me, green with seventh grade
silliness, blunt syllables flapping
in the breeze like leaf-tongues.
Silence treated me better, stilled the self
beside her, so she wouldn't detect how
I had quit the world for her sake, given up
the rabble of boys who kept their discreet
distance of one block, allowing me
the privilege of semi-private romance.
At the corner, I blessed her books gently back
to her, said goodbye, and felt separation
turn with her and nudge me away like
a sacrifice. On Barthman, I climbed stairs
to our apartment, landscape disappearing
with each step, sky filling my eyes
with diamond-bright sorrow.

In high school, I found polished floors,
low ceilings, and a sixteen-year-old girl
who told me to unbutton my shirt. She
said she wanted to mend the dead button
that hung like a fish eye near the collar.
One afternoon at three-thirty, the shirt fell
from me in the back parking lot where faculty
cars had already pulled away from spring
shadows, leaving us behind with hesitancy
and my sweat-stained shirt. She hung it
over her arm, and we walked like a married
couple down Koebel Road. It gave me some strength
to be half-naked beside her, knowing
her fingers hungered through silence
to replace my shirt with a touch.

A crewcut boy at Ohio State, I
thronged the night with other fireflies. Summer
ideas spread out on a bed that creaked
with longing. Often I blinked into oblivion,
then re-dressed, meeting no one worth meeting
again, emerging from one-night fire with the ash
of disillusionment sticking to my spine.

Years passed, as I attempted to hold
incidental lovers in my hands, their
faces bright as sunflowers, to trace
another person's petals to the stem,
to make from those touches a kind of first love,
otherworldly, but willing to drift down
to an eventual orbit of common sense,
the kind that in old age warms a starless
night with personal glimmerings.

From these moments, I learned to devalue
the fast kiss, the heart's trial and error.
I struggled free of the brain's fireworks and
the appeal of surfaces. I bypassed
love's conventions, the need to rush in
from work and throw down my coat and life
for someone who enters from another
room, rosy from routines learned from a wide screen,
saying, "Ah yes, you're home. Here, let me breathe
into your ear so you will believe I am
real, at least until you are out of love's range,
asleep in your favorite chair."

At this distance of years, I squint under
a desk lamp to record the history
of faceless bodies on best beds, my back
curved to the task, the taunt of foolish
touches faded. These nights, I am
fond only of skin I dream and poems
written on a legal pad, their sleepless
words the origin of love
drafted to the paper shadows of morning.

II

"...they traveled
like a matched team
like a dance
like a love affair."

from "The Snakes" by Mary Oliver

LONELY WOMAN, DREAMLESS ROOM

"She had been given a supreme gift of knowing how to write; she had not been given the gift of knowing how to live. She railed against this fate. She didn't want admiration as a writer; she wanted love and acceptance and belonging as a woman."

Jean Rhys by Carole Angier

I turn the vertical blind, see the commonplace
I am so desperately fond of. The streetlight,
a late-night driver, a shadowy tree are more
reassuring than a romance, than the hand that
always drops away from me. The more I understand
the illusion, the more I find ashes on the sheets
where somebody burned in my hands, then disappeared as
good luck does. I know I will get up
colorless as a moon, droop across the carpet
like the last bather on a deserted beach,
make coffee, stare at the world, turn my back
on the bed. Each night, I bring my body back to
its history. It is unthinkable that I am
flat on my back again, looking up at the sky,
my face in clouds, or am I seeing the ceiling
where the souls of so many nights have made dark voyages in
circles like filthy comets above me?
No, they are only unwashed stains from the smoke
of countless cigarettes. I lie and count them.
I clean them off with my eyes and make the ceiling ready for
another silvery night, for planets
and stars, to practice a real sky that will expect
nothing of me. I am the girl who has the
ability to touch what I have missed. I hold it
like an obsession that penetrates, fills me
as if I'd swallowed the sun, and I awaken
pregnant with words no man is father of.

SMALL SATURDAY

As you make the bed, morning yellowing
the hardwood floor, you ask yourself what you like
about the world. The answer is in your hands

much like the bedspread you shift from side to side
for some predetermined idea of perfection,
hoping that when it drops down from its final

mid-air fluff, it will hang equally over
either side, renewing a calm in the room.
Before you turn the corner, roomless, you

perform a task to hold time and solitude
in abeyance, to create the simplest
kind of eternity. You open a drawer,

push aside dust and outdated phone numbers,
provide room for keys and coins, learn how to leave
a much-sought space hollow, empty, organized.

KNOCKING ON SATURDAY NIGHT'S DOOR WITH A MELLOW FIST

I have found nothing substantial
in what I know of the world
to fill up the hollowness created
when spring makes me dark
with a dangerous craving for transformation.

I lie on my bed,
and the bed is as soft as water.
A lightning bug in a gold-yellow jacket flings itself at the window.
I have known this mood before.

Though spring is nothing but light
continuing to grow, to form leaves,
to fill trees with birds, here I lie
on the surface of a clear night,
needing a negotiable way to become new against the slippage of human emptiness.

Yes, I am in one of those moods.
I have known it all day,
since black clouds came
on the western rim of afternoon,
and the world got so small
it seemed to have only one face to show.

I lie across my bed, careful
not to like the lightning bug too much, careful not to press too much body
onto the all-night shadow
lying deceptively beside me
like the voice of someone I could love.

CABIN

The steam of a hound's breath rises to freeze
in near-winter darkness, meets wild geese
at a height of several hundred feet
above the back porch. I rinse a bucket,
pump icy water over my warm hand.
The hound creaks a wooden step, waits to return
to its rug-nest inside. Above the trees,
I can read the night aloud, its stars
engraved on October sky, their cold breath
carried into the cabin on the back of my neck.

I stack black logs inside the fireplace.
A bird broods atop the chimney. Its wings
echo down, greet my hand, encourage me
to strike the match. The hound waddles to the
hearth, noses out a spot and folds its legs
down to sleep, its ears closed to the tiny
beast atop the chimney in black frost.

I pull a second match from its paper cover.
I tell my memory to leave you
alone. I'm not going to get a good night's sleep
if I reach over to pull the emptiness near me
and find myself saying, "Where in Jesus' name
are you?" Before I can strike the second match,
I push out a quick laugh, recover
the silence, my breath shaping clouds
the size of small white roses in the cold room.

I raise my hand to light a lamp, but stop.
I want nothing to slur the firelight.
As if to break free into the cold room,
it bushes out orange as an autumn sycamore.
Its flames stumble and fall, settle down, nip
at the firescreen, roll back toward the logs.
I take off a football jersey, lock the usual
doors, pull back covers, and fall asleep
on a bed where sheets are covered with snow.

BONFIRE

An orange nucleus, open eye on the snow, watches.
Its radial sight crawls outward to phantom skaters.
Chrysanthemums of snow spew from their edges.

Beyond the starburst of silver illumination,
emptiness waits like a wolf on its haunches, ready
to tear at the quiet throat of night. Another log.

is politely fed through teeth of smoke. A tongue of heat
licks it out of a gloved hand. A winter geyser erupts,
surges upward, spirals orange-yellow-white, burgeons
bright

as a flamboyant flower overlaying the sky and moves
onlookers backwards, yet beckons. It's hot light erases
them from themselves and roars high with the glow of a
gasworks.

Hissing, popping, its static stare penetrates, blinks out
a spray of red sparks, dimly crosses the dark expanse like
love. A hypnotic craving for closeness surrounds.

I look up at the tower of flame, at the range of shadows
flickering on faces grown distinctly leafy from firelight.
I dream I was born a thousand years ago tonight.

Without touching hands, we form a circle of strangers,
a neighborhood of dreamers halfway from the fire,
deliberately silent on the circumference of cautiousness.

OPPOSING LIGHT

I snap on a lamp, too early, out of habit.
Light mantles my desk, calls ceiling,
walls, furniture into place. I am
not too tired to notice deliverance
on the outside, the other light,
the youthful shyness of April's afterglow
on the edges of trees.
I sit spectacled, trying to write,
watch the lamp outwit the artistry
of early spring. Out the window
I see what is left of dingy snow
and logs in a pile I didn't get to.
I have a craving to see a lagging snowbird
on a ravished twig, to feel the warmth
of the lamplight, an open book in my hands,
every page radiant with winter.

AUTUMN CONDITION

Easy sky, so easy to address
because it is the eye's only landscape,
enormous today, fermenting
a sparkle of birds, a clamor of leaves.
A tender falling in here. The skin
of the earth sags, brown as a donkey.
With a look over my square shoulders,
I see nearly two dozen tress pooling
in a September rinse of sun.

I used to be angry at the wasted
tenderness of autumn, at the dying
that slowly reddens up the earth with
a fever that unbuttons desire
a little at a time as if it were
a silk shirt slipping to the floor.

I used to be angry at autumn,
thick at its center with pungent sweetness,
its body of freshly cut wood and clouds
burning like sun, darkening
against me as bare as the shadowy
beat of another person's heart.

RITA RESISTS THE WEEKEND

Her hours get longer tonight, filling
with twice as much life time. She seeks
abandoned space, corners, the farthest
places away from the center of herself.
She sweet-talks her own ghost, its life
more real than her own, as it follows her
from room to room. She appeals to its
pointless thoughts that melt into her ear
from an icy tongue. She squeezes down
against the wall, against the chill
of cold paint, hunching to invisibility,
discovering an economy of existence.
Her hand climbs air to a table, tickles
a wine glass into fingers. She blinks
into its reflections, tips it onto thirst,
relaxes, ready to talk to strangers.
The empty glass hangs upside down,
its stem between her fingers. "In the shade
of trees," she thinks. "In the shade..."
then rolls her eyes to the walls, saying aloud,
"This isn't summer. There are no fields
behind me flat with the sun, and it surely is
too cold for winter." She rises, staggers
to the bedroom, slumps onto her bed to sleep.
In the morning, she swings her legs
from patterned sheets, opens curtains,
brightens the kitchen with yellow nods at dishes
in the sink. Yesterday's wine stains
remind her of last night's easy rescue.

She tugs on a shirt, jeans, intercepts
the hammering in her head with aspirin,
its white powder drying on her tongue like a wafer.
She whips a cloth from a drawer, resurrects
the queasy rooms with a little polish.
She snaps on the sweeper. Its light skims
the carpet, detects Sunday in all directions.
She pushes it back and forth, redeems
cleanliness, drawing in the dust of Saturday night.

AN OHIO FARMER THINKS THE AUTUMN WIND IS HIS WIFE

Leaf bones transparent in tin light, minor
birds, left with frost on their songs, blacken.
The bodies of garden vines coil cold. Each
day, the sky fills with the voices of the dead,
and the dying of the young becoming
old. He accepts the ancient cycle
shading from plenty to nothingness,
goes to his bed, shovels back covers,
and lies down alone, not satisfied
until he finds her in his head, alive
as a living voice, prowling his skull
against gales of October frost.

GENTLEMAN CALLER

"Like some archetype of the universal unconscious, the image of the gentleman caller haunted our small apartment..."
Tennessee Williams, *The Glass Menagerie*

Her mother hides behind a creased fan
she has made from half a sheet
of the evening news. She blushes
the whole time. Laura, her daughter, looks
hopelessly around the room, identifying
the spaces where her mother has imagined
the gentleman caller might stand, sit, search
the ceiling for something useless to say.
She fills with sighs. Her eyes scan fresh curtains,
polished furniture, newly washed walls,
preparations she has seen wasted before.
Her mother and brother, faces as blank
as white napkins, serve each other
generous portions of silence. Their
fingers trace crystal water glasses,
lift glinting silverware, shift food around
on real china plates until it becomes as cold
as paper. Tom, the brother, is mildly
intolerant of his mother's sudden chatter,
a sound more hopeless to him than any decay.
Nor does he tell her during this precious dinner
to hush or to empty her head of dreams.
Instead, at the acceptable moment,
he excuses himself, backs his chair away
from the table, and heads out the door.
Behind him, he knows mother and sister
will soon cast off the second silence,
replace it with the scraping of dishes
and discreet but shredded excuses.

REDEMPTION IN A HOTEL ROOM

for Jean Rhys

The slightest light
of a bracelet-sized moon
sulks against her scented gloves.
Hope dims to a cheap brooch
studded with artificial tomorrows.
Icy feathers of pain spread through her chest.
The liquor burns
like a deceptive lover departing
down an intestinal street.
It is quite like an old time
to get down on this back-street bed,
soaked in a cheap whiskey imitation of herself.
First, however, she insists on washing her hands.
She wants to hold moonlight on her palms,
immaculately.

THE MELANCHOLY OF FIRST VACANCIES

Among books and shelves of stillness, she adjusts
to phone calls from friends who speak of her loss
as freedom. Divorce complicates her body,
causes a weightless sway of limbs,
a miraculous mellowing after habit.
In a leather chair, she curls her legs under,
loops a comforter around her shoulders,
sips a little wine. Through the blur of glass,
she sees two faded paintings, endless walls,
misplaced love. Condemning the cadence
of slow hours chimed from the grandfather's clock,
she refuses to think of marriages
made of moon blossoming in laurel trees
or the myth of being a wife forever.
She pulls quilted warmth close, watches
firelight stray to where his presence was once
as common as breath. The room collects
winter silence from frost-bound windows.
Slipping beneath resignation, she begins
to heal in sleep untouched by a husband's hands.

EARLY MORNING BASKETBALL

I stand barefoot on the cold boards
of a rented cottage in Maine, watching
his hand flutter points upward, the brown ball
reflecting a dull shine as he tips
it over the surrounding rim of morning,
the score it earns falling out of the sun
through a web of flimsy strings. I study
orbits he makes within painted lines,
steps he waltzes into before he poses,
springs, hands like a hair-trigger,
the ball darkening the sky in the arc
practiced as the path of a bird.

I remain hidden, in undershorts,
my body whiter than ice, chilled with watching,
wondering what is the matter with me
so serious that makes me want to see this boy
jump in the air as if awakened
by water, that urges me to study
the way the ball rests in his touch.

I believe I rise at this hour only to look
at his silk movement, to see him zig-zag
with the thinnest sun over his head,
his face starting to glisten sweat
from this little dance. He is like any
boy who shines a memory into middle age,
making a grown man momentarily fear
the unconscious design he is caught in,
the getting older in the window
while sleep waits on chilly sheets
and youth, he can no longer rival, springs
from earth for briefest moments,
pressing a hunger for two points.

III

"I was even thinking a little about the future, that place
where people are doing a dance we cannot imagine,
a dance whose name we can only guess."

from "Nostalgia" by Billy Collins

THE OLD DIE OUT OF EVERY FAMILY AND LEAVE US WITH DEEP RELIEF AND USELESS REGRET

One motionless day in December
you lean against the bannister at the bottom
of stairs that lead to their rooms. You know
they are dying in beds on hardwood floors
above you. Powerless arms, withered
at their sides, have turned to ash.
You climb upwards, perhaps for the last visit.
The failing wings of their bodies lift them
to face you, perhaps for the last time.
You turn off the light too soon
and leave too casually,
as if they were only frayed scarves
flung carelessly over the backs of chairs.
When you are ready to descend
into the part of the house that lives,
you pause on the first step and hear them
disintegrating behind you like rotten cloth
ripping away from your guilty caress. Shame
takes you down the stairs. You sit
on the bottom step, looking for a reprieve.
A window above your head blares winter.
Bone chips of light choke on dust
that settles beside you. You stare out
at the way it has ended.
The numb furniture stares back. Cold
shadows hang in the hall like blackened vines.
The din of stillness immobilizes you.
It is impossible to say
that this silence is not noise.

GRANDMOTHER GROWN OLD

A hand, almost stone, on the icy
edge of agedness, traces
a welcome. I accept
the touch. I hold its skin
as if in a handshake, its veins
shifting patterns within my grip.
When I release, I feel them roll
out of my palm like sighs.
My grandmother seems suddenly
pure to me, all her world
cleansed by years spent filling pies
with berries and emptying scrub
buckets from the back porch,
refilling them with hot days.
Beside her now, nothing changed,
I help her out of a chair.
Skeptical of heart and breath,
she scuffs toward the house, enters,
presses against the sink,
and fills an old coffee pot
with water from the spigot.
Scuffling to the window sill,
she aims the spout over a plant.
I lean with her and watch
the water etch a path
in the soil. She turns. Again,
her hand shadows the plant
as if it has found a favorite spot.
She gently brushes away
waterdrops cupped on the plant's leaves.
Her careful hand pats soil
closer to the stem, securing life
with the silence of her wrinkled fingers.

AUNT ADA'S APPLE PIE

The dough in her hands
is as sultry as summer. Boldly she
squeezes, scoops flour up
from the cutting board,
silkens it into a smooth ball.

As she kneads, a glance out the window
sees a storm hanging in the distance,
heating up like an over. Her oven
has its own weather, racks worn
from holding homemade food for so many
daily meals, so many holidays. She has loved
this stove for more than fifty years.

The pie, of course, is improvised,
one of a kind, yielding the same
perfection each time without interference
from a recipe. From the drawer beneath
the sink she wields an old-fashioned rolling pin,
floats it across the powdery dough,
lets no weight touch down, but somehow
flattens the dough with less
than half a dozen flirtatious hand movements.

Then she lifts the dough into the air. It flaps
slightly, like an elephant ear, snowing flour
as she centers it over a glass baking dish.
With a surgeon's touch she presses
its softness into place around the edges
of the dish. She pats it as she would
the arm of a friend, then on the fingers
of one hand balances the pie plate, turning
its edge against the gleam of a paring knife.
Excess dough drops onto the sink top
like a white, cookie snake.

Apple slices
that still taste of an overcast morning
shingle into the bottom dough layer upon layer,
like white blossoms. She covers the mound
with another circle of dough, bonds it
to the lower one with a two-fingered pinch.

Finally, she forks holes into the top
and places the pie
onto a tongue of stifling heat.
She looks at the clock.
As if time were the last ingredient
she must account for,
she wipes her hands on her apron
and closes the oven door.

AUNT LIZ IN EARLY MARCH

She wears her dead husband's cardigan,
light wool, ragged, gold as dandelion.
She buttons it halfway down from the top,
stops at the fifty-year-old stove, stirs
homemade vegetable soup. Putting the spoon in
the sink, she picks up a scrub bucket
by the back door. The handle clangs
on the galvanized rim without warning,
the raw metal sound of her ambition,
a servitude acquired during the thirties.
Soon, she is back, brisk from the outdoors,
a rough flush flattering her face, gasps
disclosing her damaged lungs, pulmonary
fibrosis webbing inside her
like a decayed doily. Chucking a piece of firewood
onto the throw rug, she blows warmth
into her hands. I taste the cold that swirls
in behind her. Exclaiming how wintry
it is, she wings a log onto kindling
arranged like a nest. I put down my book
and watch her outline bend at the waist
to prod the fire. Nothing has changed
over the years. For her, the harmonies of work
sigh from every move, warm the room,
distract me from the chill of her decline.

HAMMERED ICE

I resist the sound of her blood,
slide to the edge of my bed, waiting
to hear a splash of fear in the kitchen
sink. On ghostly feet I glide up beside
my aunt, encircle her waist with an arm
to steady her weakness as the second
mouthful flowers onto porcelain,
spreading designs like smashed chrysanthemums.
In a scurry of urgency, I risk
leaving her long enough to retrieve
a bag of chopped ice from the freezer.
With almost closed eyes, she reaches a hand
for cold chunks, desperate medicine
discovered months ago to curb red trails
rivering from damaged lungs. Panic starts
when I see no mouth-size pieces. Melting
and refrigeration have reformed chips
and slivers into a solid mass.
Skipping steps, I speed to the basement
and rip a claw hammer from the tool rack,
a routine practiced over several years.
Back upstairs, I wrap the plastic bag
in a kitchen towel and raise the hammer
above it. In redeeming blows I bring
the hammer down upon the humped towel,
imagine white sparks inside flashing
layer by layer from stubborn ice, pulverized
now to smooth coldness. I stop myself

in mid-attack, unwrap smithereens
and scoop a cupful into her waiting
palms. She pushes them into her mouth,
eyes frantic that cold will come too late
to congeal the lacy blood spotting her
pajama top like death's corsage.
                                                    I talk
to her through this, words laden with hope.
In line with the kitchen window, I glance
at black reflections that see us give up
the safety of quilted covers
to prevail one more time against a moment
when a hammer blow will fall too late
on futile ice and Fate's indifference

AT THE END OF STRAWBERRY SEASON

My aunt rises from the waist up,
crookedly sidesteps hills and furrows,
and pitches slightly forward for balance.
Though her basket is only half full,
I can see she has finished picking
and has decided to dump her berries
in with mine. Hiding her oldness

from myself, I bend in a different direction,
and with a stereo headset covering my ears,
listen to Sweeney Todd slash ethereally
through London. While I straddle a new row
and pick another quart, I pity him
and the dreadful fate of most people.

She is heading back to the barn
when I straighten up and think I hear her heart
slowing down like the sun marking orange lace
in the sky. Just before she disappears
around the corner, I notice the weakness
in her eyes, seeking a safe place to surrender.

IMPLICATIONS OF LIGHT ON THE THIRD SATURDAY IN OCTOBER

Watching crisp sky crack open
with endless sapphire submitting
to conspiratorial warmth, autumn,
like a fist in the stomach, awakens
me with its resume of existence.
Under a Scotch pine trimmed up to the shape
of an umbrella, I work crumbs loose
from a slice of bread for robins. God knows
where they hide, clawed tight to limbs, but I know
they wait with avarice and caution and will
come pecking as soon as I disappear. Back
in the house, silence and thinner
light carpet the living room, change
the way I consider overstuffed chairs,
lamp, sofa. I open drapes wider,
become wrapped in high polish of morning,
hold nothing equal to days boasting chilly
sun across a crowbar-hard blue sky.
It is the weekend before Halloween.
In the kitchen, an uncarved pumpkin sits
on the sink top. I take the paring knife
from the drawer, cut through layers of orange,
slicing sight into penciled eye lines.
Leaves curled to stunning death flutter like foil,
hit glass behind me. I punch out
a triangular nose, square off five teeth,
coax out a ragged smile. The watery-raw
smell, wet on my fingers, goads memory,
and I see again my purchase made near

dusty cornfields, shocks bunched like autumn
effigies shadowing heaps of miniature
suns sold at roadside. I roll the seedy
insides in newspaper, carry the carved face
to the living room window sill.
In a few hours, cinnamon incandescence
will flicker outside to the few leaves left
in clusters, russet shadows holding them
to trees against absences deep as apples
dropped into the dark of orchard grass.

THE NEW THANKSGIVING

I speak to those who are absent from the room,
tell how strange it feels to pull a chair out,
realizing no one will see me
take my place at the table. I wish
I could say that the women who made a kingdom
of this kitchen are not missed. I wish
I could say that I have not lost something
of myself in their absence. This year,
no aunts or mothers carry polished silver
or porcelain cups and saucers from the sideboard
or talk nonsense, and too much, backed by gauzy
outdoor light that marks the time ethereal.
I have used up the days of family. Singed
pie crust and seasoned turkey dressing
have darkened to artifacts of another generation.
On the top shelf of the hall closet,
a linen tablecloth folded too many times
and flattened into a department store box remains
untouched, its wrinkles deepening.
It is just an ordinary afternoon in winter.
Outside, the unforgettable raisin color
of the sky of my boyhood has disappeared.
This year, the weightless weight of light straining
through the dining room window webs my shoulders,
teaches me loss through the gray of memory.

THE ANNOUNCEMENT

It is drizzling rain as you shift gears.
From street to street, the black asphalt thickens
with shiny leaves. Leaf piles at curbs form
an October border. You steer your secondhand
Civic around Columbus, its headlights
less than bright, its power borrowed against
the promise of one last tune-up. The disclosure
that you have AIDS rides like an unwelcome
passenger on the seat between us.

"At the appointed time," you start by saying,
"I will not rise again, brush teeth, buff shoes,
waste looks in the mirror." I cringe at this
sudden outburst that would seem less true
if kept quiet. "What will happen," you say,
"is nothing. Pure whiteness, that's all.
A blizzard of silence filled with the
peacefulness of a currier and Ives print."

While we coast to a stop inside
the red reflection of a traffic light,
we catch ourselves laughing at the preposterous
image of eternity amid such quaintness.
You downshift, stop at a crosswalk, silent.
We have more to say than we say.
Perhaps that is why it seems ruthless
to keep our mouths shut yet artificial
to open them for jabber. On down the street,

you slow the car, scrape tires to a stop
against the curb. We grin at each other,
an old habit to obliterate the fact
that neither of us could ever judge
the distance to the curb or to oblivion.

EVERYBODY'S LADY

Death, slender in the hips,
arms, braceleted decadence,
hikes the strap of her shoulder bag
higher, hesitates at open car windows.
People ride by with their lives
on upholstered seats, slow down,
sometimes stop, negotiate for passion.
Her trollop's mouth purses,
pink like a winter sunset,
slightly opens,
relaxes slightly,
the lower lip wet.

She fades back, saunters away,
her body as composed as ice,
as sinuous as smoke. She slinks on,
daring to nudge the night,
hand in hand with neon.
On the corner, she pauses
to pat her coiffed hair
into the look she has perfected.
With arrogant sensuality she haunts
the streets, ultimately sparing no one,
seducing the unwary
of what remains of life.

HOW THE MESSAGE OF DEATH RUINS A HOUSE

I cannot stand these large rooms,
their lost furniture, their unsmiling windows
after death. My bony heart picks through
memories. The stubborn jaw-set of
my skull resents the underpinnings
of this horror, the white smell of space,
disguised as lilac, comes out of sofa cushions.
The absence was always waiting like walls
or hunching in corners, planning all along
to silence us with its silence. Why
is there never enough time to prepare
for this violation of habits? Why
can't I step back from these moments, opening
in my chest like a time-lapsed fist,
and resume changing sheets, or water a few easy
flowers? Why must I listen to this
insult to life, sensitized to keenness
that lets me hear plaster crumbling
and wicker chairs springing apart with graceless
echoes and inelegant endings?

TIRE

You bent a finger, hooked your last cigarette,
fumbled it like a lame bird from its
cellophane nest shortly before midnight
on a Saturday. Your thumb and forefinger
pinched together the almost severed halves,
and after several drags, that very
cigarette threatened to drop its dangerous
head into your lap, so you tossed it
like a diminutive, unwanted star, out
the speeding car window. At the same time,
your left rear tire balloon-popped its breath
through a throat-sized hurricane hole, then
bogged down heavier than a hundred
buckets of wet sand. You cursed aloud.
The car mad-danced to a stop.

You opened the door, dropped to your knees
like a priest, not to pray, but to wing the lug
wrench until it spun like a silver
propeller. One lug nut after another
fell into your hand like horse chestnuts
from black autumn branches. It was
when you raised both arms to remove the tire
from its wheel that the oncoming car tore
into your blood and bones. With less resistance
than tall grass would have offered, you crumpled
to the bottom of your life without a chance
to wonder why you couldn't hold yourself
together the way you had held together
the halves of your last cigarette.

THINKING OF HART CRANE WHILE CROSSING THE ENGLISH CHANNEL

The Avalon, rooted to the bottom
of underwater calm, knocks against
fog. Lights along corridors live
like stars, accept me aboard, guide me.
I watch from the stern as the ageless
water takes me away from a land I have
barely known. The night breeze spills
shadows across my face from an island
of trees. I stand at the railing, look
down, feel the temptation to hurl myself
toward an unknown world, white jacketed
with foam, a black tie of night at its
throat. I want to accept the hypnotic
invitation, to answer death wave by wave,
to let the sea I love break over my body
so deep it would be only another shadow.

KAMIKAZE

A Japanese pilot unbelts his pants.
The tireless surf advances. He looms
over the tideline, a watercolor brushstroke
in a washed-out painting, fragile white.
It has been a sweltering day. He is dying
for a swim, yearning to ditch his shorts
and smash into the breakers. With an innate
rhythm he slams bare-assed into the hot
waves. He surfaces, his young teeth shining.
Though there is always a hint of death
in this kind of hiding place, he relaxes,
swoons with the water as it sizzles in moonlight.
He digs deep for motion. Long forward strokes
bring him ashore. Sea-black surf drains
from his shoulders. Waterdrops ripen,
start to roll like beaded silver. He shakes
them off, flings his nakedness at the moon
with the same abandon as someone
who has already lost tomorrow.

SPECIAL TRUCK

An American Greeting Card
truck bounces from pot hole to pot
hole as it passes slower traffic.
On its left rear door a rose,
perpetually alive in metal
soil, grows redder from brake light
reflections. Its petals are windproof
and will be years older before
they peel from their mobile garden.
Its beauty is stenciled to endure
and probably cold to the touch.
Drivers manipulate into
tailgate positions, desiring
to be closer to what does not die.

THE OUTSTANDING RED LEAVES

Burnt, with a blue sky closing in,
a thousand leaves on antler branches
slash the brassy afternoon, throated in
wind-swallows cool as primeval tundra.

Fiery medallions show their palms, fortunes
without futures veined in sparrow-high hands
laid out on a ledge of October air.
Elegiac sun traces doubly dentate
maple inlets where frost will soon drift ashore
in a white boat, creamy with winter's mark.

It is impossible to stop the tree
from burgeoning as if for spring. Falsely
promised an unlikely season, its blades
and midribs curl blood beauty inward,
axles loosened from steeple heights,
shrugged off from haunted limbs
like the lyrical decay of lost chances.

In the crimson canopy, in the bark
from which settlers extracted black ink
and cinnamon-brown dyes, autumn strains
to be preserved. It crawls up each branch
like a beggar in a wool sweater, snagging
a last measure of late afternoon. Hot
light sheathes petioles, margins, and

deception. Overhead, the scald of
hope, red as tongue, fails, its Indian summer
magic a temporary partner
reluctant to dance a few more days,
its steps slowing, its faces flushed
with the ruddiness of death.

ROADSIDE MORTAL

I grow orange, oxidized by four o'clock
windshield reflections. Cows drip sun, flick the
excess from their tails. Plump milkweed ash scatters
before it is touched. Tribal leaves gather,
war painted, dance a zigzag step, a zigzag step,
charge the wind like perfect warriors. To the south,
heavy with the sky's weight of blue, clouds
stoop low, show the white of their spines.
Birds with an artist's skill color the air.
The flash of their wings, a sequence of sparks,
fluctuates. They find a secret exit and disappear
before the eye can translate distance. Everything
outside is united within me. Rocks, wilderness,
the non-blinking spider's eye gouge my brain
with enormous existing. Out there, day moves on
and the emotions closest to the body glow
like the shine of wheat.

On such a day, I deliberately think of the dead,
their coffin darkness, their total absence from
a world alive with details. It is a relief to stop
the car, a great victory to open the door and be
certain I have not vanished.
I'm referring to the cold relief I feel
as I step to the ground and find the grass
still turning to light.

About the author

R. Nikolas Macioci earned a PhD from The Ohio State University, and for thirty years taught for the Columbus City Schools. In addition to English, he taught Drama and developed a Writers Seminar for select students. OCTELA, the Ohio Council of Teachers of English, named Nik Macioci the best secondary English teacher in the state of Ohio.

Nik is the author of two chapbooks:

- Cafes of Childhood
- Greatest Hits

as well as eight other books:

- Why Dance
- Necessary Windows
- Cafes of Childhood (original with additional poems)
- Mother Goosed
- Occasional Heaven
- A Human Saloon
- Rustle Rustle Thump Thump
- Rough.

Critics and judges called *Cafes of Childhood* a "beautifully harrowing account of child abuse," but not "sentimental" or "self-pitying," an "amazing book," and "a single unified whole." *Cafes of Childhood* was submitted for the Pulitzer Prize in 1992. In addition, more than two hundred of his poems have been published here and abroad in magazines and journals, including *The Society of Classical Poets Journal, Chiron, Concho River Review, The Bombay Review,* and *Blue Unicorn.*

He won First Place in the 1987 National Writers' Union Poetry Competition, judged by Denise Levertov, First Place in The Baudelaire Award Competition, sponsored by The World Order of Narrative and Formalist Poets (1989), Second Place in *Zone 3*'s first annual Rainmaker Awards, judged by Howard Nemerov (1989), and Second Place in the *Writer's Digest* annual competition, judged by Diane Wakoski (1991).

Acknowledgements

Cover design and art: Elric R. DeVault

The poems in this book have appeared in the following publications:

*Amelia, Ariel VIII, Back Home in Kentucky, Byline, Cutting Edge Quarterly, The Devil's Millhopper, Fennel Stock, Gypsy, Half Tones to Jubilee, Impetus, Kentucky Poetry Review, Lake Effect, Mississippi Valley Review, Muse, Negative Capability, The New Press, Outposts Poetry Quarterly (*England*), Painted Bride Quarterly, The Panhandler, Phoenix, Poetpourri, Poetry Durham (*England*), Pudding Magazine, Shorelines, Slant: A Journal Of Poetry, Stone Country, Success Magazine (*England*), Success Poetry Anthology (Success Magazine) (*England*), Sunrust Magazine, Third Lung Review, Wind Magazine, The Windless Orchard, Writers' Journal, Zone 3*

www.ingramcontent.com/pod-product-compliance
Lightning Source LLC
Chambersburg PA
CBHW010139030826
48979CB00023B/1044

* 9 7 8 1 7 3 4 9 4 6 9 1 8 *